Living With...
Allergies

Nancy Dickmann

Consultant: Marjorie Hogan, MD

BROWN BEAR BOOKS

Published by Brown Bear Books Ltd
4877 N. Circulo Bujia
Tucson, AZ 85718
USA

and

Studio G14, Regent Studios,
1 Thane Villas, London N7 7PH, UK

ISBN 978-1-78121-802-0 (library bound)
ISBN 978-1-78121-808-2 (paperback)

Library of Congress Cataloging-in-Publication Data available on request

Text: Nancy Dickmann
Consultant: Marjorie Hogan, MD, Professor of Pediatrics, University of Minnesota, Retired staff pediatrician, Hennepin Healthcare
Design Manager: Keith Davis
Children's Publisher: Anne O'Daly

Manufactured in the United States of America
CPSIA compliance information: Batch#AG/5651

Picture Credits

The photographs in this book are used by permission and through the courtesy of:

Front Cover: Shutterstock: Kzenon;
Interior: iStock: caracterdesign 20, SeventyFour 20–21;
Shutterstock: Stephen Barnes 22t, Rob Byron 16, fotorawin 18, Elizaveta Galitckaia 18–19, KPJ Payless 4, LStockStudio 12, Microgen 14–15, Monkey Business Images 12–13, Lokoolp Narongrit 16–17, NDAB Creativity 14, Pixel-Shot 22b, ProStock Studio 8–9, Y Sveta 10, Yana Tatevosian 4–5, tektur 8, triocean 10–11, Siarhei Yurchanka 6

All other artwork and photography
© Brown Bear Books.

t-top, r-right, l-left, c-center, b-bottom

Brown Bear Books has made every attempt to contact the copyright holder. If you have any information about omissions please contact: licensing@brownbearbooks.co.uk

Websites

The website addresses in this book were valid at the time of going to press. However, it is possible that contents or addresses may change following publication of this book. No responsibility for any such changes can be accepted by the author or the publisher. Readers should be supervised when they access the Internet.

Words in **bold** appear in the Words to Know on page 23.

Contents

What Are Allergies?

Do you sneeze when you stroke a cat?
Does your nose run when you're outside?
Does your skin sometimes feel itchy?
These are signs of an allergy.

Many plants produce pollen.
Some people are allergic to it.

Your body fights **germs**. They cause disease. But sometimes it attacks harmless things. It might attack **pollen**. It might attack a kind of food. This is an allergy.

How it Works

Different things cause allergies. They are called **allergens**. Sometimes they enter the body. Your body gets ready to attack. It thinks it is fighting germs.

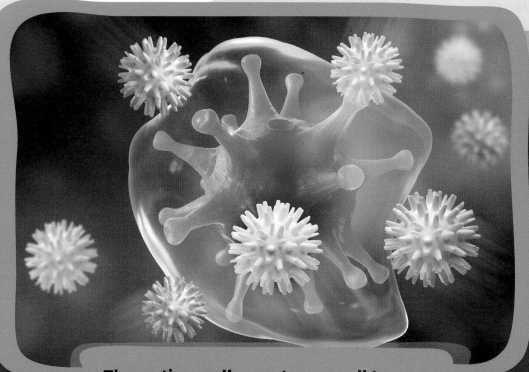

These tiny **cells** are too small to see. They help your body fight germs.

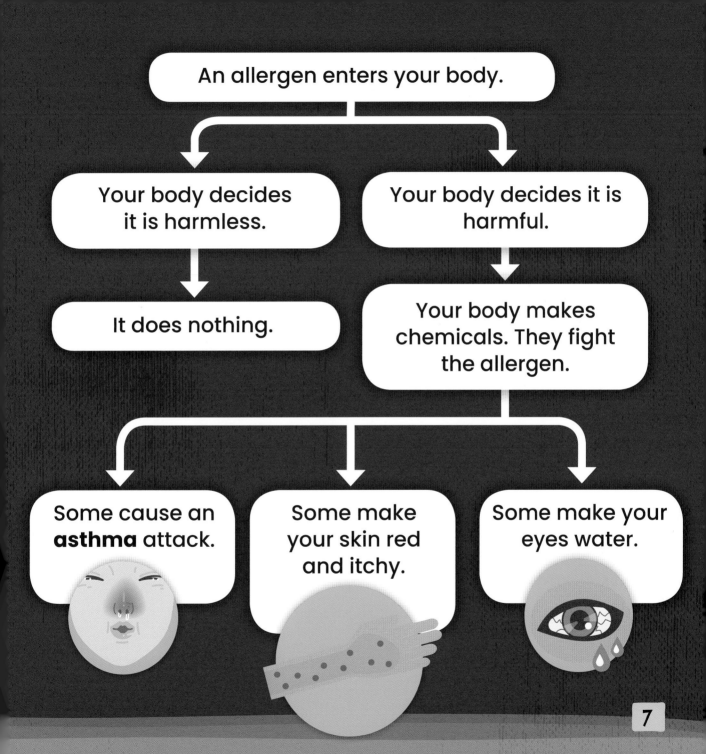

An allergen enters your body.

Your body decides it is harmless.

Your body decides it is harmful.

It does nothing.

Your body makes chemicals. They fight the allergen.

Some cause an **asthma** attack.

Some make your skin red and itchy.

Some make your eyes water.

Allergens in the Air

Some allergens are in the air. People breathe them in. They make you sneeze. They make your eyes itch and water.

A pollen allergy is often called hay fever.

People can be allergic to animals. Cats and dogs have flakes on their skin. The flakes cause a **reaction**.

WOW!

Dust mites live in our homes. They are too small to see. Their droppings are an allergen.

Food and Other Allergies

People can be allergic to foods. Some are allergic to nuts. Others are allergic to milk or eggs. Eating these foods can cause a rash. It can make it hard to breathe.

Many people are allergic to fish and shellfish.

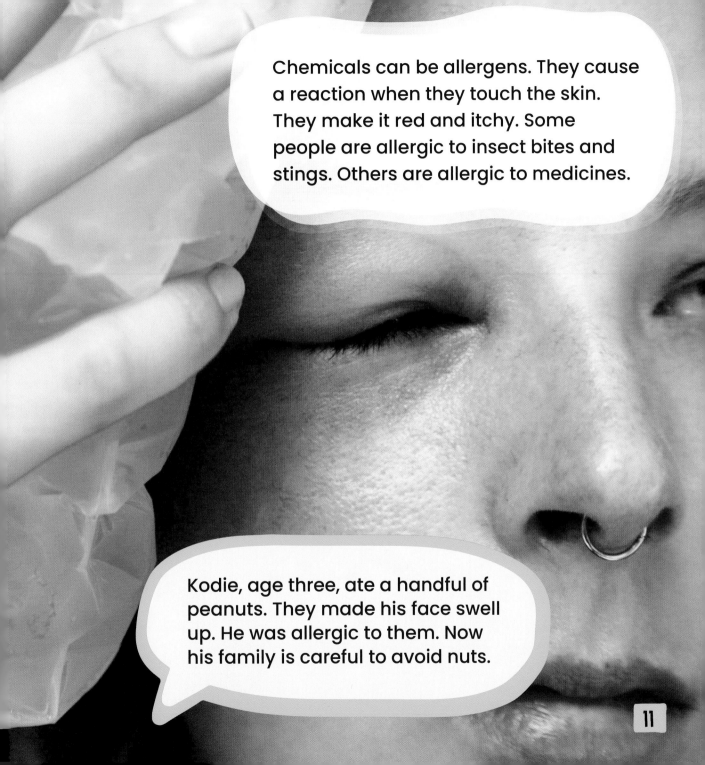

Chemicals can be allergens. They cause a reaction when they touch the skin. They make it red and itchy. Some people are allergic to insect bites and stings. Others are allergic to medicines.

Kodie, age three, ate a handful of peanuts. They made his face swell up. He was allergic to them. Now his family is careful to avoid nuts.

Who Gets Allergies?

Many people have allergies. Young children often have them. Sometimes they outgrow them. But they can last your whole life. Adults can develop allergies too.

Many children have food allergies. They are less common in adults.

Do your parents have allergies?
That makes you more likely to have them.
Why do some people have them and
others don't? No one really knows.
You can't catch allergies.

About **15%** of people in the
U.S. have an allergy.

That's about
50 million people!

13

Testing for Allergies

Doctors can test a person for allergies. They find out what they are allergic to. The doctors try different allergens. They test until they find out what causes a reaction.

Sometimes doctors take a blood sample. They test it for clues to an allergy.

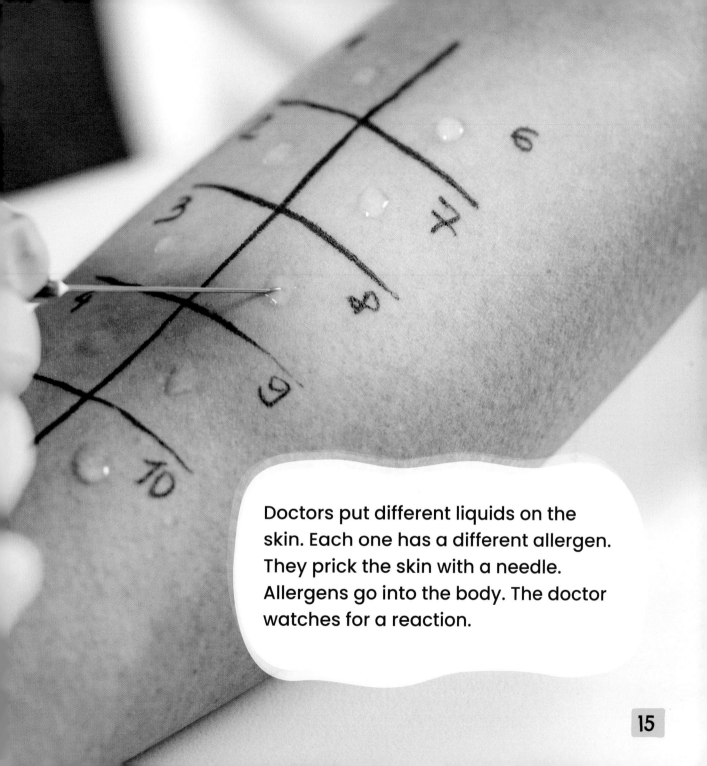

Doctors put different liquids on the skin. Each one has a different allergen. They prick the skin with a needle. Allergens go into the body. The doctor watches for a reaction.

Staying Safe

Everyone's allergies are different. They can be annoying. But they can also be dangerous. Some people have very bad reactions. They might need to go to the hospital.

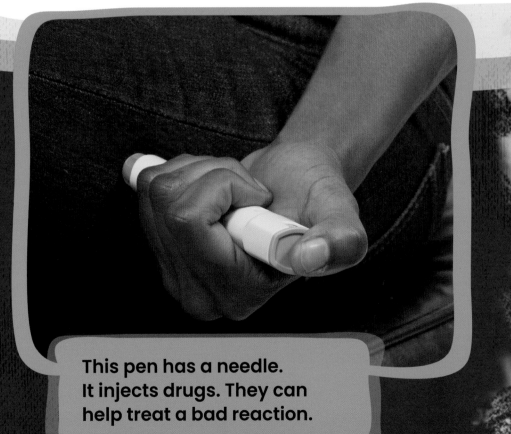

This pen has a needle. It injects drugs. They can help treat a bad reaction.

People stay away from things they are allergic to. They read food labels. They get rid of dust in their homes. They stay away from furry pets.

WOW!

Some kinds of cats have no hair. But they can make you sneeze!

Treating Allergies

Medicine can't make an allergy go away. But it can treat the **symptoms**. It can make a person feel better. There are many kinds of medicines. A doctor will tell you what to use.

Allergies can make eyes itchy. Special eye drops help soothe them.

Your body makes chemicals to fight allergens. Some medicines block them. There are pills you can take. There are liquids to spray in your nose. Other medicines are creams. They help dry, itchy skin.

No More Allergies?

Scientists have a new way to treat some allergies. It is called immunotherapy. A doctor gives a patient tiny amounts of an allergen. Each time they give a little bit more.

This is often done at a hospital. The patient might have a bad reaction. Doctors will be there to help.

The body gets used to the allergen. It doesn't react as much. This might take a few years. The allergy probably won't go away completely. But it might become milder.

Ali has a milk allergy. He tried immunotherapy for a year. Now he can drink a small glass of milk. He hopes to eat cake at parties soon!

Activity

Many foods contain allergens. People with food allergies must be careful. There are laws to help them. They say that allergens must be listed on the label.

Allergy Advice

Contains: Egg, Mustard

May contain:
Nuts, Peanuts, Sesame Seeds, Celery, Wheat, Barley, Fish, Soybeans, Milk,

Choose some packaged foods from your kitchen. Look at the labels. Are the allergens easy to find? Are they shown in a way that makes them easy to spot? How many different allergens can you find?

Next time you eat at a restaurant or café, look at the menu. Are the allergens listed?

Words to Know

allergen a substance, such as pollen, that causes an allergic reaction in some people

asthma a health condition that can make it hard to breathe

cells the tiny building blocks that make up humans and other living things

germs tiny living things that can cause disease

pollen a dust-like substance made by flowers, which plants need to make seeds

reaction something that happens in response to something else, such as getting a runny nose after breathing in pollen

symptoms the outward signs of an illness, such as a fever or rash

Find out More

Websites

aafa.org/allergy-facts/

dkfindout.com/uk/human-body/body-defences/allergies/

kidshealth.org/en/kids/food-allergies.html#catsick

Books

Fearless Food: Allergy-Free Recipes for Kids Katrina Jorgensen, Capstone Young Readers 2017

I'm Allergic to Grass Walter Laplante, Gareth Stevens 2018

Living With Allergies Michelle Levine, Amicus Publishing, 2015

Index